THE

Practice

Paul's Prayers in Ephesians

THE
Practice

Paul's Prayers in Ephesians

ARCHIE MURRAY

PRAYING BELIEVERS SERIES

THE PRACTICE
Copyright © 2025 by Archie Murray

ISBN: 978-1-4866-2217-7
eBook ISBN: 978-1-4866-2218-4

Word Alive Press
119 De Baets Street Winnipeg, MB R2J 3R9
www.wordalivepress.ca

WORD ALIVE
—P R E S S—

Cataloguing in Publication information can be obtained from Library and Archives Canada.

DEDICATION

I've met countless people who genuinely refer to themselves as "believers." I respect and love them all, and they've all encouraged me in my Christian life in some way. Some of them, not a majority, were especially "spiritually" minded. This was evident in two particular ways: they understood that God was involved in everything in life, and they prayed spiritual prayers.

These praying people reached heaven with the Bible language of prayer. They had an "other-worldliness" about them. They were victorious, strong, bold people, even though they might have been physically weak.

The others, the majority, were more like this world. Their Christianity was confined to common sense, good ideas, and human experience—not a bad set of standards, but lower than the spirituality Paul exhibits in his prayers and lower than the Bible's image of the believing child of God.

I dedicate this book to the first group for setting an example to me and others. Their prayers are similar to Paul's, which this book is about. They are special people, and it has been a privilege to know some well. God knows their names.

Contents

Acknowledgements

My love, affection, and gratitude go to the two churches I've been involved with since coming to Canada in 2003. First Lobo Baptist Church, near London, Ontario called me from Scotland as their senior pastor. I served there for thirteen years. Never was a pastor loved more and showered with so much blessing and support. I'm also grateful to Ilderton Community Bible Church, where my family and I have been in membership since my retirement seven years past. Both churches love Jesus Christ and seek to honour the Word of God and its principles. They introduced me to the beautiful, bright, and distinctly Canadian Evangelical Church. A warm, friendly, loving, willing body of believers are in both churches, and I acknowledge here their unseen, but known to God, influence on my life and family.

PREFACE

It seemed natural to include an example of real, true prayer after a study of the Lord's Prayer itself. Many prayers are recorded in the Bible. The book of Psalms, at one level, is a record of prayers. The prayers of Jesus have been widely studied.

I inclined to Paul because he illustrates an essential element of prayer that's missing from many prayer meetings in churches today, and not just in Canada! That's the element of a spiritual, biblical view of life, the world, the church, and prayer. How well I've been able to convey this while trying to maintain a simple, devotional, and encouraging message I'll leave the reader to decide.

This book isn't intended to be academic, theological, or impressive in any way. It is intended to make the reader discontented with ordinariness, especially when the topic is prayer. Prayer is simply humans talking to God. How can we have reduced this amazing, mind-blowing concept to everyday normality? God is real. Prayer is real. Can we be real too?

INTRODUCTION

This is the third book in the series Praying Believers. It's a follow-on of the two previous books, *The ROOM: Preparation for Prayer* and *The PATTERN: The Lord's Prayer*. The three books together present three helpful teachings on prayer. The first addresses the need for preparation before prayer. The second is a close look at the Lord's pattern for prayer, and the third is designed to show what the practice of prayer looks like from the example of Paul's prayers. Paul shows us the free expansion in personal prayer inspired by the pattern.

I don't intend to bind believers to certain rules or even heavy guidelines in prayer. The Lord's Prayer is certainly not a rule in the sense of being a strict law, but it does provide guidelines and structure for our own benefit. Paul's prayers in Ephesians illustrate what true prayer should look like. You'll be invited to gently examine your own praying against Paul's and his heart affection for the Lord and His people.

Ephesians is one of the grandest books in the Bible. Pauls' language, like that of Jesus, is spiritual. It lifts your spirit to heaven itself. Prayer should do likewise.

This letter, while addressed to the Ephesians, was probably intended to be read at Ephesus first but then sent to all the other churches in the wider area. The point is, this letter includes us in a very particular way even today if we are indeed faithful in Christ Jesus. Paul's prayers are naturally and lovingly interspersed for us throughout Ephesians.

Paul didn't limit his thinking to specific circumstances relating to one church. He addressed issues that relate to the general life of every church. We can regard the ideas and concerns he raised in prayer as relevant to believers praying today.

I commend this short book to you, with its companions. These are pastoral, practical, and devotional meditations on prayer. I pray that as you read, you might be blessed.

Rev. Archie Murray
Southern Ontario
Canada

Chapter 1
CONVERSATION TURNING INTO PRAYER

EPHESIANS 1

The letter to the Ephesians begins with a variation of Paul's regular introductions to his letters. It identifies who he is as "*an apostle of Jesus Christ by the will of God*" (Ephesians 1:1a), thereby declaring at the very outset the divine seriousness of the letter's content. At the same time, it indicates Paul's authority to speak. He also identifies to whom he is writing. The recipients are the "*saints who are in Ephesus, and faithful in Christ Jesus*" (Ephesians 1:1b). The issues Paul raises are timelessly relevant and therefore pertinent for us today.

An endearing characteristic of Paul's letters are his greetings. He uses greetings as a prelude to a benediction. The greeting and the benediction are like the ribbon on the gift box. They sum up all the love, concern, and affection of the sender that can't be contained or fully expressed in the package. They reveal Paul's heart for God's people everywhere throughout time.

Paul's letters are written with such passion that they can't fail to move the reader. His love for the Lord is evident in the letter to the Ephesians as he worships God, who blesses us in

Christ. He is effervescent in his glorying in God, in Christ Jesus, and in the Church. After the briefest of introductions, Paul spontaneously writes fourteen verses of the first chapter, enumerating the gospel of God in Christ and its benefits to the believer. Then before he deals with any other issue on his mind, he quite naturally and almost imperceptibly turns to prayer. The ease with which Paul moves from conversation to prayer is a mark of a man walking with God. This man is prepared for prayer as a daily manner of life.

He has rejoiced in the gospel, and when he writes about it, he's inclined to burst into prayer. His conversation is so engaged with God that prayer is a natural place for him to go. Often our prayers are mechanical, external, a segment in our busy day. For Paul, the practice of prayer was the natural flow of his thoughts, emotions, and intentions. Prayer should be the Church breathing. Breathing responds to the stimuli of life in the natural man. Every situation in life should produce prayer in all of its variation for the praying believer.

The gospel for Paul is not merely the best philosophy the world has ever been given. The gospel impregnates his entire being. He loves it, everything about it, and everyone who is likewise enchanted by the gospel of God. His prayers reflect this spiritual fervour.

All of these principles working in Paul's heart lead him somewhere. Paul moves from introduction to greetings to worship and then naturally to prayer. Ask yourself as you read: "When was the last time I heard anyone pray like this?" Do you pray like Paul? You can. Prayer is a natural response from the life of God in the soul of the believer to the normal and extra normal issues of life. Minute by minute, hour by hour, day by day, until that day when Christ returns!

Notes

_____

_____

_____

_____

_____

Chapter 2
PROMISES PRAYED

"Therefore I also, since I heard of your faith in the Lord Jesus and your love for all the saints, do not cease to give thanks for you, making mention of you in my prayers" (Ephesians 1:15–16).

If you follow the pattern of the Lord's Prayer, you'll see that Paul has been influenced by its general character and content. He's not bound by it like a set prayer. He's free but guided in principle.

See the commitment Paul is ready to make to pray for God's people: *"I do not cease …"* Thankfully, only heaven knows how many false promises are made on the subject of prayer! Paul doesn't just give an empty promise in the name of Christian kindness. He looks back over an unspecified time to the day when he heard of the Ephesian church. From that day he continued to prayer for them.

For Paul, praying wasn't just a matter of discipline, or even a commitment kept. His consistency was fed by faith and a real sense of the power of prayer to change things we cannot change. Yet his actual prayers have nothing to do with changing circumstances. They're about changing the Church. Paul's faith generates such an energy that he prays what he believes is necessary for them to walk with God in a like-minded faith.

This "*making mention of you*" is the level of his honesty, not a subtle confession of failure. It's a distinct assurance that they've been spoken of before God on significant occasions right up until he pens the epistle. He's talking about a present part of his regular praying. As Paul writes to them, he is praying for them! But Paul isn't content to stop at that; he wants to give them assurance beyond doubt. So he proceeds in the following verses to tell us what he prays for them.

Paul shows a distinct disinterest in the mundane issues of daily life, despite the fact that for him they were regularly anything but mundane! Paul understands the formula:

To Live = To suffer

Chapter 3
INFLUENCE

"... that the God and Father of our Lord Jesus Christ, the Father of glory ..." (Ephesians 1:17).

In prayer, it's not what you know but who you know that counts. Here you are instantly translated to a different kind of praying. Pauls' expectation of prayer is shown in his desire to speak with this most powerful being we call God, whose credentials and power to save are exemplary! He takes the time to make much of the God in whose presence he prays. This is the "Hallowed be Your Name" of the Lord's Prayer. Paul exalts Gods as he tells us who he's been talking to about us. He manifests the glorious names of God, as much as to say "Do you see who I've been talking to on your behalf?" As Paul raises the Ephesian church and makes mention of them, he tells them whom he's speaking to!

Can you catch the glorious power of such praying? Do you see how it instantly glorifies God? Do you see the importance Paul attaches to these Ephesian brethren who, as far as we can tell, he'd never even met! He had only heard about their faith. In prayer ...

It's not what you know but who you know that counts.

Jesus told us that His Father was interested in sparrows. (Matthew 10:29). The point isn't that sparrows are important but that God cares about everything in His creation. But Jesus didn't tell us to pray for sparrows! God's care is extended even to the unknown, without fanfare or pleading. We can rely on His daily care for many things we don't expect to happen and for many things that do. God's care often happens without us needing to prompt Him as though He was sleeping.

Paul describes God as "*the Father of glory.*" His prayers begin with worship, reminding himself, and them, of whom he's addressing on their behalf.

So he has told them who he is and to whom he is praying. Now he tells them what he's asking for. We should listen and gently compare our prayers for our brothers and sisters. There's something about Paul's prayers here that's missing too often from our prayer meetings. The aim of this little book is not to discourage but to encourage a higher interest in each other in prayer.

Chapter 4
THE SPIRIT OF WISDOM

That He *"… may give you the Spirit of wisdom and revelation in the knowledge of Him"* (Ephesians 1:17b).

This little clutch of words enhances the previous points. Our Father is not limited in what He can give. He can shower gifts of all sorts and sizes, all types and kinds, all levels of worth. What do you want from Him today?

Too many want riches; too many want fame. Too few want what Paul asks for. Solomon is famed for this request (1 Kings 3:9–12), and no doubt Paul, the pharisee of the pharisees, knew this. And so he prayed that they might have *"wisdom."* But he calls it the *spirit* of wisdom. He's not talking about book knowledge.

Book knowledge is good, but this is better. Wisdom is good knowledge warmly understood in the context of real life living and applied to real events. It doesn't make the possessor proud. It doesn't make them rich. It makes them harmless to the innocent and trouble to the trouble maker, just by their wise words. Wisdom doesn't need a sword, but it might require a shield. Wisdom is both when required.

Paul prays that these believers might have wisdom. This is an essential for believers in a hostile world, and there's no other kind of world—only varying degrees of hostility.

I wonder how the Ephesians felt when they read this? How would you guide Paul to pray for you? Could you improve upon this standard of care for the believer in this world? Perhaps you'd hurry on in your reading, hoping for something a little more tangible! This spirit of wisdom is significant because it indicates a quiet, unseen, imperceptible influence that is often the effective character of the spirit of wisdom applied.

Paul writes "*spirit*" with a small "s." He's not referring to the Holy Spirit specifically, but it is holy and undefiled, pure and powerful. It attaches itself to the believer as a gift from God and is a developing, growing attribute in the believer's life. It's attractive and Christ-like to all who recognize it, as in "*Never man spake like this man*" (John 7:46b, KJV), and "... [they] *wondered at the gracious words which proceeded out of His mouth*" (Luke 4:22a). I feel sure that you would like someone to pray such a blessing on you! Pray that Paul's prayers will be answered in your life!

Chapter 5
A BEAUTIFUL SPIRIT

"… and revelation …" (Ephesians 1:17).

Paul chose his words based upon his own experience of living the Christian life. The Christian life begins with a revelation from God to the sinner. This revelation opens his eyes and he sees and understands the things of God for the first time. It reveals the world as God sees it, and he sees himself as God sees him. He recognizes who Jesus is. Though he might have known all about Jesus for years, now he sees Him through eyes of faith that have been spiritually opened. We don't discover God, as His ways are *"past finding out!"* (Romans 11:33b). God discovers Himself to us.

Paul prayed that this revelation would fill their hearts and minds and colour life and reality for them, that they might see the world through God's revelation to them and forever depart from its ways. This revelation is first and foremost a revelation of God. But like a new suit shows up the old shoes, the new man sees the discolouration of everything else. This man becomes separate from the world and its ways, not just from its extremes of wickedness but from its "spirit." This revelation sets men apart for God.

Some believers when they begin to understand a little theology become proud. They imagine that this gift was not a gift at all but their own learning. They think that their own research brought them to this place of understanding. This is a failing in many. Such an attitude hinders the free flowing of the gift of wisdom and the revelation of God. They become arrogant and brittle. Hear James commenting on this very point: "*But the wisdom that is from above is first pure, then peaceable, gentle, willing to yield, full of mercy and good fruits, without partiality and without hypocrisy*" (James 3:17). What a beautiful spirit and revelation Paul wants for believers then and now. Pray for this revelation for your pastor , elders, deacons, church workers, parents and teenagers, and every other category.

Chapter 6
KNOWLEDGE THAT PRODUCES CHARACTER

"... in the knowledge of Him" (Ephesians 1:17b).

Paul is praying for believers, that they might have wisdom and revelation from God. He also asks that they receive these two qualities in a particular way: *"in the knowledge of Him."* That is, the Lord Jesus Christ. Everything Paul prays for is brought into the character and spirit of Christ. *"In the knowledge of Him"* seems to suggest that everything we receive should be brought into contact with the "new man in Christ" within us. So that there not be any conflict, they may be brought into subjection and under the influence of the Christ within us. For example, work out this principle when you choose a life partner. Weigh the potential person in one hand against your knowledge of Jesus Christ in the other. If they don't balance, then you have a decision to make. You shouldn't need to pray agonizing prayers for "guidance." The knowledge of Jesus Christ Paul speaks of will enable you to make the right decision.

The *"knowledge of Him"* means knowing Jesus so well that we know how He would use such wisdom and revelation in the daily dealings with this world and in the church and family life. Our knowledge of Him was initially a revelation, and that revelation must colour all aspects of the believer's life. Oh that God would answer Paul's prayers for the Church! Perhaps you might pray such prayers for the Church. You know that pain and sorrow will go away soon because life is short. Eternity is long; it will never end. Paul's prayers make a difference in time and eternity.

Would such character in the Church not make us stand out from the crowd? The world falls apart around us. There is a crying need for such gifts to manifest in believers' lives all over the world. There's a desperate cry for such a revelation of Christ in the Church. Such is Paul's burden for the Ephesians.

His prayers for us stir the same desire within us today—that prayer governed by the spirit of Christ Jesus might emanate from us in our private and corporate prayer times and produce a wise and gentle Church that understands what the will of the Lord is.

We also must understand the role of the Church in the world, as it's still a powerful influence today and a terror to evil-doers. We need to be empowered by the call to take the gospel of Jesus Christ to every person. What did you want Paul to pray for you? He has only begun to pray. His prayer is a spontaneous development from a letter that began with praise identifying the God he serves. His prayers reflect, consciously or unconsciously, the pattern Jesus laid out for us in the Lord's Prayer. This is the Kingdom of God coming—an army that knows how to use its weapon, its "sword," the Word of God.

Chapter 7
LIFE'S DARK NIGHT ILLUMINATED

"the eyes of your understanding being enlightened ..."
(Ephesians 1:18).

Paul is still not ready to pray for "bread." He sees a more important need for enlightenment in the believers in Ephesus. This need is not due to a problem but due to a condition—they aren't yet fully grown in Christ. They're still in the process of developing the "new man" within. Peter says similarly, "*but grow in the grace and knowledge of our Lord and Savior Jesus Christ*" (2 Peter 3:18a). Paul recognizes our tendency to decide that we know enough already and to stop learning, growing, and developing. We stop seeking enlightenment from God's Word and Spirit.

Such is the case with many. They have arrived at a place of self-satisfaction. When they look into James's mirror, they come away forgetful. They feel they have no more growth left in them. Paul prays for them. This enlightenment is specific in its subject matter.

The subject matter Paul is praying for can only be had by the enlightenment God gives by His Spirit. This is yet another gift. You can't sign up for a course on this enlightenment. Many think they've already graduated, but Paul doesn't think so!

Enlightenment is a relatively simple word. Here in Ephesians 1:18, it's used metaphorically for spiritual enlightenment. The apostle John, writing about Jesus, says "*That was the true Light which gives light to every man ...*" (John 1:9). He means that Jesus lit up the world when He came to it at His incarnation and during His life, death, and resurrection. The writer to the Hebrews writes about his readers as having been enlightened, or illuminated, by the gospel of God's grace (Hebrews 10:32).

Enlightenment can be gradual or sudden, but it's never superficial. It's always sufficient for the moment but always to be sought after for more. It's not just a clearer understanding but like a blind man receiving his sight—life changing! But he now has to learn to live in this new world of different obstacles. Paul is talking about a fresh and perpetual opening of our eyes to see Jesus, to understand afresh the simple gospel story that we thought we had fully grasped many years ago!

Paul prays for them to receive this enlightenment. How easily the old gospel truths become jaded. The angels are amazed! But the believer begins to stiffen and dry up the moment this love story begins to lose its thrill. When it no longer moves us to tears, we lose our ability to care for the lost. When Calvary doesn't reduce us to silence, we forget repentance and become immune to sin. When we don't give thought to His cross, we lay down our cross. When the Church stops talking about His love for us, we stop loving one another. When we're no longer sufficiently excited to recount how we were first enlightened, when we forget who led us to Christ, when we're no longer interested in fellowship, then we've gone back to the dark, cold world and are a mere shadow of who we really are—the children of God. The world becomes an even darker place. Paul's prayers might still be answered in us, but it will take a work of God's Holy Spirit in reviving power to change us. This is why Paul prays thus.

We must not forget how dark the night of our life was when the light of the glory of God shone into our hearts and we saw Jesus. Paul recounted his testimony, and it's recorded in the book of Acts for us to read. Three times the busy Bible record sets out the conversion of Saul of Tarsus, the apostle Paul, in Acts 9, 22, and 26.

It appears from Paul's prayers for the Ephesians that this forgetfulness must be countered by fresh enlightenment by God's Spirit. The Church is always being refreshed when it's vibrantly testifying to the grace of God. When the Church preaches a clear gospel message regularly, its members stay enlightened. When churches hide behind such statements as "The gospel is found in every page of the Bible" (which is true, but not as they present it), they begin to view the simple gospel story that saved them as being too simple for their advanced state of understanding. And then they die. They may continue to indulge in esoteric theological ramblings, but they will die spiritually. It's hard to imagine the church at Laodicea contemplating the sufferings of Christ and sharing the testimony of how they were redeemed by His precious blood. But it's easy to imagine them musing over finer points of doctrine. It's also easy, and much more enlightening, to think of the Temple sinner Jesus spoke of walking daily in the Saviour's love.

Having said all this at length, note that it's our *understanding* that must be enlightened. This is not just an emotional high but a growth in understanding from study, teaching, and/or diligent Bible reading. Emotion alone isn't honouring to God in someone who should know better. Much of present-day church life is either mere frivolous emotionalism or all head knowledge. Such enlightenment must regularly be tested to refine it and remove the dross of empty emotional and/or intellectual indulgence. Paul goes on to deepen this explanation and affirm it as a real thing to be experienced.

Chapter 8
The Life-Changing Power of Hope

"… that you may know what is the hope of His (God's) calling"
(Ephesians 1:18b).

Paul just keeps taking us deeper into the Christian experience. He wants the Lord by His Spirit to enlighten us and make us know *"the hope of His calling."* What does he mean?

Paul uses this word "know" with a clear sense of its meaning and as it has come to be understood throughout the Bible. Paul wants us to know the hope of God's calling intellectually and, more pertinent to his praying, he wants us to experience this hope in terms of its influence and effect on our daily life. Paul has experienced this hope as a life-changing power.

He prays for the Ephesian church and for us today, that this hope of eternal life in Christ, and all that is implicated theologically and biblically in the word, will be experienced in daily life. So what is the power of this hope? Listen to the absolute assurance Paul has of his hope in Christ: *"For this reason I also suffer these things; nevertheless I am not ashamed, for I know whom I have believed and am persuaded that He is able to keep what I have committed to Him until that Day"* (2 Timothy 1:12). Note the effect this hope has on Paul in his tangible, present experience: "*I also suffer these things, nevertheless I am not ashamed.*"

Paul's present suffering is a direct result of his hope in the gospel. Yet he suffers gladly and is not ashamed. If his hope was futile, then shame would be the correct response to his foolishness in believing it. But his hope is not futile because the hope itself is so sure that it fills him with the tangible power to rejoice in suffering.

Ask yourself how you pray for your family, friends, and church. This is biblical, empowering praying. When we understand and see this hope as an inward spiritual reality, other things are set in order of precedence. My present problem is reduced in significance in a healthy way. It's not simply disregarded, like a stoic shutting down his mind and body, but I apply a comparison chart to my life experience at every level. On one side is the believer's glorious eternal hope in Christ. On the other is a lot of temporal issues that make this life challenging. There are extremes that often appear, but in terms of priority and focus, the praying believer understands this conflict. He sees things in the light of eternity. Seeing life in the confines of its physical term is short-sighted for the believer. Paul wants the Lord to open our eyes, to enlighten us to see the hope we have that is invested in eternity. This hope has its power and source in eternity. It's a gift from our Father in heaven. Eternity is the praying believer's realm now!

When you leave your old job for a new one, there may be issues remaining that have to be dealt with and addressed seriously. Anyone who has done this just wants them resolved so they can get to the new place. That's like the issues of this short life against the hope of God's eternal calling.

Notes

_____

_____

_____

_____

_____

Chapter 9
AN ETERNAL INHERITANCE

"... and what are the riches of the glory of His inheritance in the saints" (Ephesians 1:18c).

This is where Christianity, in its fundamental truths, shows its real power in the lives of believers, hence why Paul prays for the Ephesians to know the riches of the glory of His inheritance. What is this inheritance? The word takes in the whole gospel. It is God's inheritance in the Church, as a bride for His Son in eternity. It's the believers' hope of eternal life in Christ for all eternity. It's the hope of eternity in heaven itself, with God our heavenly Father and His Son, our redeemer, and the Holy Spirit, our helper who empowers us to live the Christian life. These are eternal hopes, and we have received them in significant measure in the gift of the Holy Spirit. He is the primary, initial deposit of the gospel hope. That the believer actually experiences this in-dwelling of the Holy Spirit gives him sufficient power to live and overcome in this short life.

We are privileged to be able to emulate Paul's praying. His experience is spiritual, and his understanding is that the gospel is spiritually beneficial in the natural realm. It lifts the believer out of the natural world and provides spiritual impetus to overcome the world. This strength is illustrated in his prayers.

The inheritance is the fulfillment of all the purposes of God in time and eternity. Does this not echo the beautiful, concise statement from the Lord's Prayer, "Your Kingdom come. Your will be done on earth as it is in heaven"? Paul understands this and expands the concept, filling it out and thrilling us with its grandeur.

Chapter 10
POWERFUL PRAYING FOR POWER

"and what is the exceeding greatness of His power toward us who believe, according to the working of His mighty power"
(Ephesians 1:19).

This verse shows Paul's application of the truth he has expounded on and prayed for, that they might experience God more and more.

One element of the text will give us a grasp of the enormity of Paul's prayers for us and the need for such prayer to become the norm among us for each other. It's the phrase, *"according to the working of His mighty power."*

The Church today in many places is earth-bound, content, and with no real spiritual experience. There's nothing of note in its accomplishments. We accomplish little more, and often less, than an enthusiastic charity. Our interests, vision, and activities are often earth-bound. Were we to suggest that God could provide for our new building quicker, cheaper, and more willingly than the bank manager, we'd be quietly dismissed, ignored, and perhaps even laughed at. Yet the profession we make is that God Almighty attends our meetings in person! That He is all powerful. Of course He's not our servant, but Paul prays that the

Church might experience God in reality. Hear his heart as he bursts into praying for them and us, that we might know what is the "*exceeding greatness of His power towards us.*"

Paul is so overcome with the glory of God in His work in us that he strives for the most profound and extravagant language to express what he knows is available to the Church as individuals and as a community of believers. This is true faith-filled prayer. This is prayer that gets answers. This is prayer that glorifies God and will revive the Church and lift it to a higher level of existence in the world today.

Our children will want to attend this church's prayer meeting! They'll want to experience this living God in our midst as they hear their parents and seniors glory in God's great name. They'll become strong in Christ, confident in their beliefs when they see their parents as living examples on their knees and knowing God. Pray like this for yourself and every believer you know. This is prayer that will bring in the Kingdom of God. This power of God is toward us, says Paul. It's for us. It's for you.

Here Paul returns to the content of his communication with the Ephesians. He imperceptibly turned the conversation to prayer, and now he returns prayer to the conversation. Paul seems to move gently out of praying and begins with his initial and similar energy to share and teach about this power. It's the same power He wrought in Christ when He raised Him from the dead! Does this single sentence not stir up faith?

Even the remainder of this passage is impregnated with this power. God honours Paul's speech, his writing, his heart-felt longing to see the church at Ephesus living in the power of God. This is not Pentecostalism! This is Pauline! This is the heart of God Himself for His people being expressed by Paul in prayer. Prayer must be a reflection of God's will, not ours! Follow Jesus's pattern and Paul's example here and God will honour your prayers. This is Kingdom praying!

As a tail piece, see the exhortation of the old apostle John to the Ephesian church of his day. He is exiled on the island of Patmos for his faith in Christ. He sends a message to the church in Ephesus. In it he strongly warns them of an error that has crept in among them that must be expunged by a faithful return to the source of the Church's life. He says:

> ... I have this against you, that you have left your first love. Remember therefore from where you have fallen; repent and do the first works, or else I will come to you quickly and remove your lampstand from its place ..." (Revelation 2:4–5)

Notes

Chapter 11
THE POSTURE OF THE PRAYING MAN

"For this reason I bow my knees" (Ephesians 3:14a).

Here again Paul begins to pray. See the character he ascribes to the praying man. He bows his knees. This has been the posture of the praying man for centuries, right back to ancient times. Kneeling is a statement. It says, "I am less than the one I address. I respect him. I may even be afraid of Him. I adopt a posture of weakness and vulnerability, thereby acknowledging my inferiority. I submit. I worship. I am willing and ready to obey." That is the attitude of prayer.

Posture says a lot of things about us. Onlookers observe and take note. Sometimes they simply form an opinion without reasoning it through. Other times they realize that the praying man is stating by his demeanour something about the person he's praying to. To whom is Paul bowing his knees? He takes the time to tell us. But before we go on, this is not a new rule for churches! Mandated kneeling at wooden pews is not at all what Paul is looking for. It's first of all a heart attitude, and then it's a private statement to God alone. Then it's a freedom to express this humility in the house of God with other saints.

If your knees are worn, give them a break. If your back is sore, sit in a comfortable chair to pray. God is not taken with externals! However, He knows that hearts must find visible and physical expression for their passions in every other area of life, and the kneeling saint before His God and Father is one such expression. This has been a characteristic of the Christian Church for centuries. My fear is that its absence in many churches today, even in prayer meetings, may be a revelation to us of the state of our hearts' affection for Jesus Christ. Paul is praying for you and me. He wants us to be like him so that we may be as blessed as him.

Chapter 12
BELONGING

"… to the Father of our Lord Jesus Christ, from whom the whole family in heaven and earth is named" (Ephesians 3:14b).

Paul clearly states who God is. This is again Jesus's pattern in action: Our Father in heaven, hallowed be Your name.

Here he includes the whole Church in heaven and earth, which is named from Him. What a wonderful sense of belonging Paul has as He prays! It's similar to when Jesus brings us to our Father at the outset of His pattern for prayer in the Sermon on the Mount. Do you have that sense of belonging? If you don't, discover why quickly. Prayer, while addressed to God Almighty, is never desperation. It is always to our loving heavenly Father. Having a loving heavenly Father but also desperation makes no sense—or shows no faith!

Many people lack this sense of belonging in the modern Western world, despite our social justice, social engineering, and social programs. Sadly, despite our churches' claims to being family, belonging is not a word that instantly comes to our minds when we think of church. Many full-blown active members of churches today see no one from the body of Christ between Sundays. Their neighbours are their helpers. The Lord has to send the "ravens," the unclean birds of the air, to help them because they, like Elijah, are alone. The warm, kindly friendship that pervades the church at Sunday morning "worship" evaporates in the noonday sun and we go home empty and lonely, not having this sense of belonging that Paul eludes to. The situation is generally circular, of course. More often than not, we are largely to blame for our own lack of belonging.

Paul counters this negativity. He says we belong to the whole family in heaven and on earth. The evidence is our name! We are the "family" of God! The individual believer who prays for the Church daily, like Paul does, will not feel alone. They will identify in prayer with other believers and make them their life's focus. This may initially be in simple deeds of kindness, thoughtfulness, love, and care. But in a short space of time, God will draw you into the fold of the love of His family, and your name will become known. The Church must not forget to do good. Paul writes to the Galatian church, "*Therefore, as we have opportunity, let us do good to all ...*" But he adds a priority: "*... especially to those who are of the household of faith*" (Galatians 6:10). Charity begins at home. It's often more noticeable when we give to our enemies, but God sees it more when we give to our church family members first.

Paul understands that praying for someone opens your heart to them, and when you give them your Christian affection, fellowship, and interest, it will be reciprocated. So these are the things Paul asks our Father for on our behalf.

Chapter 13
NOT OUT OF, BUT ACCORDING TO

"that He would grant you, according to the riches of His glory ... "
(Ephesians 3:16a).

This is interesting language. What is it to grant someone something? A grant is a gift toward a need with no requirement to be repaid. It's free. It affects a change in providing the opportunity to do something or have something you wouldn't be able to have otherwise. It assumes fulfillment and is akin to free grace. What is the grant for? This grant provides what believers need to live the Christian life. They need to be strengthened with might through His Spirit in the inner man. This grant will enable that.

The grant is given "*according to the riches*" of His glory. Now this is a subtle distinction. To be given a grant merely out of a bank account doesn't tell us enough. It could be $1 out of a $1,000,000 bank account. That grant bears no relationship to the total value of the account. To be given a grant "according to" means it's based upon the value of the account. In other words, the size of the account determines the size of this grant! And in this case, it's according to the riches of Christ! See that unbounded extravagance in Paul's prayers for the Ephesian believers. He is generous with his affection for them. Pray like him for your brothers and sisters, and you will become generous like Paul.

This extravagance of faith should be a regular component in our prayers for one another. Paul is illustrating by the power of his prayers the power he feels the church needs. Without prayer for such strength, we will fail.

It is inner strength. This is the strength of the steel girders that are the hidden structure of our buildings. Real strength is deep inside of us and is only visible when stress comes. It surprises those who thought they knew us. It's a gift of the Holy Spirit. Paul wants us to be strengthened with might. This doubling of the request highlights the need for this strength.

I imagine that many believers think they have no need for strength and might combined! But we do. God the Holy Spirit is waiting to hear you ask; then He will give such help in trouble. Have you ever thought that the Lord didn't understand your difficulty? Paul knows He does, and Paul knows the Lord will answer this prayer, which may seem extreme in its expression. Paul and the Lord both know what the problems of life are like!

Many believers are living lives in weakness because they live in ignorance of the Holy Spirit's power. Our Father knew the battle we'd be in. He knew we wouldn't survive on our own. We need the Holy Spirit's power daily. We can know His help if we seek it. His work is to lead us to Christ. His work is to strengthen us in our walk in the world. Pray for one another. We all know, like Paul knew, how hard it can be. We need to pray for this grant of Holy Spirit power for our brethren and sisters. This is a whole different category of subject matter from what we experience at many church prayer meetings. Prayer meetings would be full if this was the content of our praying. And God would answer. See how close to the purposes of God Paul prays.

Notes

_____

_____

_____

_____

_____

Chapter 14
HEARTY FIRESIDE PERMANENCE

"that Christ may dwell in your hearts through faith ..."
(Ephesians 3:17a).

Paul is talking to believers. This seems like a strange request. Surely he means that we might sense this reality more acutely. For many people, this refers to a background truth with very little experience. Paul wants the Lord to bring this truth to the surface in our lives. You might know believers who are quiet, distant, and hidden in their walk with the Lord. They need this Christ to dwell in their hearts in such a way by faith.

The claim that Christ lives in me must be accompanied by some evidence in life. How can we be so insensitive to the Lord that we never talk to Him? How can we be members of the body of Christ yet never pray meaningful prayers, like these prayers of Paul, for one another? Our energy is spent on the trifles of ill health and lost jobs and mortgage payments while the Kingdom of God is under attack and God's will is resisted. We need to know this experience vibrantly—Christ dwelling in our hearts by faith. This again is Paul praying "Your Kingdom come, Your will be done."

The word "dwelling" carries such a hearty fireside permanence. How do we attain this experience Paul prays for us? We achieve it by faith: *"this is the victory that overcometh the world, even our faith"* (1 John 5:4b, KJV). Faith is an active agent in the believer's life. Faith and prayer live in an interactive synapse. They support each other.

Pray for your brothers and sisters who fail to exhibit such a relationship, that they might be restored to a real walk in the Spirit. Paul understands the essentials of the believer's life: personal prayer for ourselves, private prayer for others, and community prayer for us all to know Christ dwelling in our hearts by faith. While it gives this confident assurance and power to serve, it also provides that warm fireside comfort in the evening after a busy day facing whatever life threw at you. We are never alone as believers and even less alone when we pray like Paul, when we take time to prepare to pray, and when we follow Jesus's guidelines in our praying, however generally. We are most connected when we follow the pattern as Paul does here in the letter to the Ephesians.

Chapter 15
PLANTED

Pray as Paul prayed: *"… that you, being rooted and grounded in love"* (Ephesians 3:17b).

Often love is an airy, light, uncontrollable, and superficial emotion. The love Paul prays for is substantial. It's our roots attached to firm ground. It doesn't move around with every wind of doctrine, nor is easily led astray. It stands in the storm unmoved.

The love Paul talks of is reliable, trustworthy, pure, innocent, harmless, but powerful to save. Paul envisages a revived Church, a passionate Church. A Church that loves one another. It is not afraid. It is strong and gracious We should pray like Paul and let this vision colour our praying for our brothers and sisters. Pray for these things for one another. We should be discreet in public. Private prayer, however, allows total freedom.

In our private rooms in isolation, we should be able to pray freely in the Spirit for one another, and especially in these terms. Pray then like Paul prays, that we be rooted and grounded in love.

Paul understands these characteristics as necessary to comprehend the love of Christ. See Paul's reasoning for the necessity of such spiritual prayers.

Notes

_____

_____

_____

_____

_____

Chapter 16
INCOMPREHENSIBLE DIMENSIONS

"[That you] *may be able to comprehend with all the saints what is the width and length and depth and height—*"
(Ephesians 3:18).

We need help with this word used in the NKJV, "comprehend." Seeing the need for enlarging on the meaning, the ESV clumsily says, "*the strength to comprehend.*" It's better translated to "attain," but even that needs some enlargement. It means grasping something. The Greek word *katalambano* means to attain, in the sense of making something one's own. Whether physically or mentally, it means appropriating something, securing a prize, even obtaining something.[1]

These words come together in English to tell us that Paul has something significant in mind when he says that being rooted and grounded we might be able to attain, to comprehend the love of Christ! In verse 19, Paul restates his thought, saying that you may be able to "*know*" the love of Christ. He uses the word "know" in its fullest sense. Have you experienced the love of Christ? If you have, you'll pray passionately for everyone you

[1] W.E. Vine, Merrill F. Unger, et al., s.v. "attain," *Vine's Complete Expository Dictionary of Old and New Testament Words* (Camden, NY: Thomas Nelson Publishers, 1985), 44.

meet, that they might also know the love of Christ. This is the example of the apostle Paul and is seen when Jesus guides us to pray "Your will be done on earth as it is in heaven." Surely comprehending the love of Christ is to be discovered there in the pattern.

Paul desires this experience for the Church so much that he can't contain himself. He says that having a firm foothold on life, rooted and grounded, you might be able to grasp the fullness of Christ's love, in all of its *width and length and depth and height.* Is there anything in life bigger to contemplate, let alone comprehend?

Paul is thinking of the universal Church in the world, wherever they are. He sees the Ephesians as part of something much bigger than themselves and much greater than the Roman Empire and the history of Israel. The Ephesian church is part of the Kingdom of God in Paul's worldview. The Church is the Bride of Christ. We need to pray that our brothers and sisters can comprehend this.

What inspiring prayers Paul shows us! What an exciting enterprise our prayers should be for one another. The church's prayers in private and in the corporate prayer meeting are about the gospel of Jesus Christ and His love and redeeming grace.

This is not intended to dissuade us from praying about our current hospital appointment. However, dear believer, to limit prayer to physical ailments and the normal problems of life, no matter how serious, suggests that we have a problem of priority and faith. Paul had many problems, physical and mental. Real enemies. Jail time and near-death experiences. Yet his prayers for the church don't include these matters much, if at all. There were no hospitals, no emergency care, no drugs to take, yet he doesn't pray for a miraculous deliverance or ask others to do so. He prays for spiritual remedies. Every problem for Paul was eased by being close to Jesus. This is true for us and all of our believing friends. So learn to pray like Paul.

Notes

_____

_____

_____

_____

_____

Chapter 17
LIFE-CHANGING LOVE

"to know the love of Christ which passes knowledge ..."
(Ephesians 3:19a).

Paul prays that we may know Jesus's love, which passes knowledge! Paul's prayer thus is the result of living thus. Every day Paul walks with Jesus. He speaks about Him and leads people to Him. Then he prays that they might know Jesus as he himself has come to know Him. Paul prays what he believes. Believe and walk by faith.

Paul isn't afraid to pray for the impossible, that believers can know that which passes knowledge! This reveals a lot about Paul to us. His heart and mind are filled with deep desires that can't be fully delineated. They are mysteries of the spiritual life of the believer. Paul is also grasping at the biggest blessing he can imagine for these brothers and sisters in Ephesus, and surely right into the future to us today. Paul wants God to make you special. What kind of praying is this? Is this not a heart bursting with the love of Christ that passes knowledge?

This affection for Jesus Christ generates Paul's energy in praying for the Ephesians and us. Use him as an example. To what end does Paul pray these things? That we might be filled with God. This concept is yet another extravagant request. It is Paul's heart's desire to see the Church filled with the love of Christ, a love that's beyond understanding. Paul wants us to "know" it. He's not talking about an intellectual grasp of theological principles. These might help us express it, talk about it, or explain it. But Paul wants us to feel it, to experience it in the deepest sense, in a life-changing way. Like he has.

Chapter 18
FILLED WITH GOD

"… that you may be filled with all the fullness of God"
(Ephesians 3:19b).

Paul is filled with the fullness of God as he writes this. This is Pauline writing at its best! This is a man who knows God. This is the birthright of every believer. It is not a theological degree! It is not an ecstatic one-day wonder. Paul's very being is engulfed with the love of God in Christ. This is who Paul is. Who are you, dear reader? We testify that the same Christ lives in us. The whole world is desperate to see Him. How do we allow Him to be seen? The exact same way Paul does.

Paul's life is saturated with Jesus Christ. Jesus is not a hidden, secret part of Paul. He is visible even when Paul prays. The answer to Paul's prayer here is that we should seek the Lord for such a relationship, for this Christ-likeness exhibited by Paul as he prays in this letter. Do you hear it as you read his letters? Do you sense his desire for your life to be so filled? Does it make you want to know this fullness of God? God's desire is to fill you with Himself by His Spirit.

Prayer is where it all begins to happen in reality. Not on the platform in the worship meeting. Not listening to the sermon passively. Not reading set prayers in a public meeting. It begins in your private room in the secret place with God the Most High. Just me and the Lord hidden, and hiding, in Him. Until you covet this place, you will never know the experience of the fullness of God. That's why Paul's writing and praying is saturated with vision and hope and with an intensity of desire that you and I might respond to his heart. God is also speaking through Paul. Do you hear Him?

Paul's writings have none of the characteristics of fanaticism. They are the genuine heart experiences of Paul the "praying believer." He is so full of anticipation for you and me to know God in fullness. As he prays, he bursts into a benediction, as he already did in Ephesians 1:20. Listen to Paul's glorious confidence in Ephesians 3:20–21 as he pronounces on you this "good ending"—his benediction ...

Chapter 19
TRIPLE SUPERLATIVES

"Now to Him who is able to do exceedingly abundantly above all that we ask or think, according to the power that works in us, to Him be glory in the church by Christ Jesus to all generations, forever and ever. Amen" (Ephesians 3:20–21).

Paul prays with active faith. He is a praying believer! Never be afraid to ask for the unimaginable thing that you need to serve God. Never doubt His ability or willingness to give you more than you ask for. This is a praying believer. This is prayer that gets answers. Listen to his confident boldness predicting the answers to his prayers, announcing how God will do this. He is able to do *"exceedingly abundantly above."* What kind of language is this? It uses triple superlatives. Neither Hebrew nor Greek can give Paul one word to satisfy his need of expression. Love that passes knowledge, filled with fullness, exceeding abundance! Does this sound like a religious person? Paul is a believer. Paul is filled with *"joy unspeakable and full of glory"* (1 Peter 1:8, KJV).

He is clearly also filled with a desire for every believer to experience the Lord in the way he has. He doesn't regard his own experience as unique to himself. He doesn't imagine for one moment that he himself is special in this regard. Paul is fully convinced that you and I can and should know the power of God in our daily life. This is Paul's understanding of the normal Christian life. It's also an accurate statement of what the Bible teaches overall about the experience of God in the life of every believer.

Yet so many live in spiritual poverty. Paul knows this to be a real danger even in his day, so he prays large prayers for his brothers and sisters. We should do likewise. This is the practice of prayer, but it's never to be seen as a skill to achieve. There are no experts at praying. Just real, ordinary, faithful praying believers.

Chapter 20
POWER TO LIVE

Paul tells us how this will all happen. It will happen "... according to the power that works in us..." (Ephesians 3:20b).

This is the role of the Holy Spirit, who lives within the believer. His work is to empower us to live for Christ. The sentence "I can't do that" in relation to walking with God should never cross our lips. The praying believer is triumphant and wins the battles. He is not defeated, even when he fails! He has this power within that enables him to rise out of the ashes of defeat and fight again another day, and fight he will until that great day when God calls him home to heaven and a reward—that he knows he didn't earn! It's the reward of faith fulfilled. There is a power within every believer. Why are so many defeated? There's no excuse; no reasoning will suffice. We have the power to live for God.

The Holy Spirit is an entrepreneur! The believer in whom He dwells tries things no one else will try, and he succeeds. He goes further than those who went before him. He conquers mountains thought to be too high. Every time he falls, he rises again. His trust is in the Lord.

The Holy Spirit leads us to Christ. He sanctifies us. The Holy Spirit gives us the power to witness verbally and in manner of life. This is the subject matter of Paul's prayers for believers. When believers pray to their heavenly Father, gently influenced by Jesus's pattern, what a difference it will make to the prayer meetings! The place of prayer will be the glory of our gatherings. Christ seated in the heavens in all His majesty, being worshipped by His people in heaven and on earth. His Kingdom will be increased, and His Will will be done on this earth. His coming will be hastened. God's people will have bread. Temptation will be overcome. People will live in an atmosphere of forgiveness. Evil will not ensnare us. Pray, pray, pray like Jesus taught us and as Paul shows us.

Chapter 21
To All Generations

"to Him be glory in the church by Christ Jesus to all generations, forever and ever. Amen" (Ephesians 3:21).

The greetings at the beginning of a letter and the benedictions at the end are a unique class of writing, of expression. They summarize the writer's relationship to the reader and express the writer's affection and desires for his readers. In this they resemble prayer. They could be reasonably defined as a type of prayer. In the ending of this spontaneous benediction, Paul summarizes his desire for the glory of Jesus Christ to saturate everything he has said to the Ephesians. Paul believes that when the Church lives in a way that reflects his prayers, Jesus Christ will be glorified in believers individually and corporately. Also, he believes and prays that this experience of God in Christ will spill on through the generations of families of believers.

How many believing families watch their children leave the Lord? Many just comfortably disappear into this evil world as though a holy God had never been in their thoughts. Paul illustrates the depth of believing prayer that resists this curse. He, like us, wants to see the children of the Church follow in our footsteps and champion the truth of God into the future. We give up too easily. We capitulate to all sorts of weak, unbelieving excuses and fear. Many a parent is afraid to speak to the adult child about the love of Jesus! May God answer Paul's prayers for us and our prayers for our children. He will when we begin to pray for our children like Paul prayed for us.

Chapter 22
A GLORIOUS PLACE

You've perhaps noticed that Paul hasn't strictly followed the pattern Jesus gave us in the Sermon on the Mount. Nor has he ignored it. It's a pattern to guide, not a straightjacket to kill expression, and not the bit in the horse's mouth to pain it into obedience. It's not the thole keeping the reluctant oar noisily in its confines, but the fine paper pattern to be handled delicately, which allows for adjustments to fit the wearer. It must always be on hand and regularly consulted. The only boundary is that of common sense and a respect for the original designer.

He ends his prayer at a glorious place. He has completely passed over the need for daily bread. He has forgotten to ask forgiveness or to give forgiveness. In this, he is practically illustrating to us how heavenly prayer should be. He doesn't mention temptation or evil. Evil is far from the thoughts of the man filled with Jesus Christ. He creates such a godly atmosphere in prayer that it reduces the likelihood of temptation or evil finding a comfortable space in which to reside.

He illustrates to us the glory of real prayer. It is heavenly, Spirit-filled, and energetic in faith, even if it's physically weak in expression. We're not all in our prime. It's bold, extravagant, and big in its vision for the people he prayed for. I wonder if Paul prayed according to Jesus's guidance when He said, "... *whatever you want men to do to you, do also to them* ..." (Matthew 7:12).

Paul is teaching about faith-filled prayer, and the present-day church desperately needs to re-learn it. Though some of the legitimate subject matter of prayer is depressing, like forgiveness and temptation and evil, the intercession for the generations of believers affected by these evils is gloriously powerful. It brings God's blessing and presence to those who go forth weeping and bearing precious seed (Psalm 126:6).

Chapter 23
PRAYER THAT WORKS

This is how to be kept from evil. This close walk with the Lord will keep you from evil in many forms. Such a walk is heaven on earth, no matter the mess. That's the effect of real prayer Paul is illustrating. Our lives in all their miserable circumstances become reflections of the glory of God in Christ and us. Your life can become the same kind of inspiration to those around you, as Paul is to us as we read this letter.

Here Paul moves again quite naturally from conversational teaching to prayer. You can feel it arising in him as you read. He can't contain himself. The more he exalts in the gospel, the more he wants to pray that it becomes a living reality in the Church. This is a pattern that works!

The gospel message is not just one of the messages in the biblical canon. It is *the* message on every page—sometimes hidden, sometimes bold, but every time we must find it. Prayer and the gospel are biblical conjoined twins. For lack of such praying, the church languishes spiritually. Hence, Paul in this prayer for the Ephesians (and us) engulfs himself in the gospel message and bursts into a most glorious, but premature, benediction. He still has a final benediction at the actual end of his letter.

Chapter 24
PRACTICAL PRAYING

Paul is not just praying; he is teaching us about prayer. It fits our narrative to understand Paul's thoughts on practical praying, though hopefully by now you are convinced that practical praying for Paul is intensely spiritual. Read what he says in the following passage about praying and think about all your experiences of prayer. Make a comparison, and be honest but not too harsh on yourself. You're not alone if you feel out of your depth when you pray. Paul presents a high standard but a glorious experience worth praying for.

While his praying is filled with spirituality, he is intensely practical, as is the Lord's pattern. Paul gives no mention to some of life's necessities in his praying here in Ephesians. However, spirituality translates intensely into the practical daily lives of praying believers. These are the people who are last to leave the church meeting and first to serve others. Praying believers are valued by their society and workplace for their diligence, and they're loved by those in trouble because their prayers are translated into personal commitment to the gospel of Jesus Christ and the teaching of God's Word in the Bible. They are a blessing to the world that hates them. This is Calvary love. This is the love of Christ shed abroad in our hearts. Pray for this to be the daily experience of your brothers and sisters in your church and for the Church universal in Christ.

Chapter 25
BATTLEFIELD PRAYING

In Ephesians 6:18a, Paul says "*Praying always with all prayer and supplication in the Spirit …*"

Here, Paul destroys the idea of a ten-minute time of prayer being sufficient for daily devotional. He says "*Praying always.*" If you've ever learned anything, you know that time is a necessary commitment to success. Lack of time is a commitment to failure. Paul has in mind a life of prayer, a lifestyle of prayer, a constant state of being in prayer. Always means always. Surely our present-day churches have set us a very low expectation in prayer! Few attend, even fewer pray. Those who do are often accused of praying too long or being boring. Yet a round of golf takes five hours! Paul says "*Praying always,*" and he doesn't intend it to be a monotonous drone through a prayer list. Prayer for Paul is an exciting and glorious privilege.

There are legitimate cases for ten minutes of prayer, as long as it's backed by a life of prayer. But ten minutes a day will leave you weak and ineffective as a believer. The person who develops a life of prayer will be able to pray for as long as time allows. This is a hearty exhortation to energetic, serious, battlefield prayer. How we view the world and our life and purpose in this life will affect our praying, not just in how much time we spend in prayer but also in its energy.

Paul sees the world as a passing vale of tears, richly to be enjoyed and in which to have a life that is fulfilled in serving God. Paul tells us about his sufferings, but they are transient to him. They don't move him, and he never gives up or loses heart, even when hearts are failing all around him, because he sees life as a battlefield, a war to be fought. This has to make him difficult to live with. He was a warrior with a cause. He sees the cause of Christ as ultimate sacrifice. He loves that principle and sees his sufferings as in Christ. Grasp this warrior spirit and you will approach life events differently and succeed. This is the practice of prayer.

Chapter 26
SUPPLICATION FOR ALL

"… being watchful to this end with all perseverance and supplication for all the saints" (Ephesians 6:18b).

Here again Paul pushes our reluctance to experience prayer at a different level with a different dynamic. It takes diligence to pray like this. Be vigilant, be watchful. Supplication is very alert, very energetic. It has stamina and power. Sorry, but it often takes more than ten minutes! The perseverance of the saints is evidence of their new life in Christ. They don't quit easily. They don't tire easily. In the midst of the challenge of time and commitment to prayer, Paul tells us of this essential type of praying. He calls it *"supplication for all the saints."* We must not become too persistently local in our praying. Prayer can change the world.

Paul puts everyone before himself, but he can't function without the prayers of the saints, any more than the weakest believer can survive without it. Paul needs it doubly due to his calling and duties as an apostle of Christ.

"Supplication" is a simple word that means to ask for something, preferably on someone else's behalf, but it can be for the individual themselves. For many, praying for themselves is the sum total of their experience. Paul is rounding off his thoughts and uses this general word to speak for all aspects of believing prayer. Another book would be required to go into all the ramifications of prayer. This book is just an introduction. This simple word has been abused in the modern church by making it the sum total of prayerful expression. Prayer is not just about asking for things. That is a minimalist view on the subject. Paul is concluding his previous and more full descriptions of prayer.

Paul destroys the idea that merely asking gets answers. Hear his prayer! He also makes clear that needs aren't the only things to be prayed for, as if the only "needs" of the believer are temporal or physical. The primary function of prayer is not just to get things. The horse leech cries "Give," not the praying believer.

Paul is not just asking for things as he prays for the Ephesians. He is fellowshipping with God his Father. He is sharing his heart's burdens and desires, cares and vision, hopes and fears. The myriad of circumstances in the believer's life are in Paul's prayers, but they are all gloriously presented as privileges to be embraced spiritually and overcome by faith.

Chapter 27
"I WILL PRAY FOR YOU." WILL YOU?

"and for me, that utterance may be given to me ..."
(Ephesians 6:19a).

Now Paul knew how to speak. Humility or critics aside, he must have been an eloquent and skilled communicator, trained and experienced in every circumstance imaginable. So what does he want from those who pray for him? We all want the same initial things from those who pray for us. We want them to actually pray! "I will pray for you" is such an abused statement, made often without a glimmer of intention.

Never say you will pray and then fail to pray. It's better to say nothing and then pray a lot. You've just learned the unattractive skill of insincerity. The statement has actually been robbed of meaning by the church. Why do you need to say anything at all? The benefit of praying for the needy is not to encourage them with thoughts of your prayers, even if you didn't pray. The benefit is that somebody did pray and God heard and answered. A better statement to hear would be "Did I tell you about how the Lord intervened in my life this week?"

Paul asks real people to really pray, and he tells them what to pray for him: words, expressions, the ability to actually effectively speak. Just as he prays for the Ephesians, he also wants to speak the gospel. I have wondered why so few believers today, even some professing to be missionaries, don't ask for this same thing. It's as though we've become comfortable with inability. Pray for yourself and believe God answers. Pray for your frightened brother to be so filled with faith and power as to be unable not to speak.

Chapter 28
SPEAKING IN CHAINS

"… that I may open my mouth boldly to make known the mystery of the gospel, for which I am an ambassador in chains; that in it I may speak boldly, as I ought to speak" (Ephesians 6:19b–20).

The church needs this boldness. Paul repeats this need for boldness in Ephesians 6:20, saying it is how he ought to speak. We spend a lot of time trying to make the gospel accessible to people. Paul says make it known, yes. He just wants to make it public! He wants to speak it out at every opportunity. This confidence that Paul exhibits is lacking in the Church today. Paul says speak it! Boldly!

At the time of writing, Paul is in prison. Meditate on that for some time. It's difficult in the Western world to imagine such an experience, because Paul's prison experience doesn't exist in our world. No need to expand on the circumstances. We can understand life being impossible in some way, often because others have shut our lives down. It's a universal experience and the methods are legion. The Bible characters from beginning to end share this with us. Life can be a prison in reality or metaphorically. Paul is an example of the power of God in the praying believer. That faith overcomes circumstances. Faith lifts the believer out of real circumstances and into heaven itself. It frees us from real confines and gives us freedom in the prison, so free that the worldly free man is not as free as the believer in prison. Every believer can know this freedom in Christ. Too many today are still in a prison they have painted, furnished, carpeted, and called "home." Paul is a free man in Christ. Are you? If not, learn from Paul's prayers. Go to the Sermon on the Mount. Find the Lord's Prayer and learn to pray. It can change your life.

Chapter 29
PEACE, LOVE, AND GRACE

We've come to Paul's final benediction. His last thoughts as he ends this letter. Notice that he has never strayed far from His love for the brethren: "*Peace to the brethren, and love with faith, from God the Father and the Lord Jesus Christ*" (Ephesians 6:23).

He wants us all to know peace. Paul has known peace in turmoil. The gospel experience produces peace that passes understanding. It brings peace where there is indeed no peace. Pray for all God's people to have God's peace.

Pray also that they would know the specific love Paul calls for in this benediction. The love we need is firstly love with faith, a love that believes God is and that He loves us. This understanding of love, impregnated with faith, is what to pray for your brothers and sisters. It is divine love.

In Ephesians 6:24, Paul writes, "*Grace be with all those who love our Lord Jesus Christ in sincerity. Amen.*" God's love brings grace, free and unearned favour, and not just when you think you need it. This grace is always there, always freely available, being shed on you daily if you're a believer, and in measure even if you're not. Grace "*be with*." That's a constant, not haphazard or merely on demand. It's constant grace given to all those who love our Lord Jesus Christ. Do you love Jesus Christ?

Paul must sadly qualify this condition of loving. It's only to those who love "*in sincerity*," a genuine, real, felt, expressed, and lived love for Jesus Christ. Not a mushy emotion but a real force in your life that leads to God first and then to your neighbour. Paul knows that not every professor is a possessor. Make sure you are the real thing: "… *Believe on the Lord Jesus Christ, and you will be saved* …" (Acts 16:31).

Paul teaches us how to pray by praying. He exhorts us, and his exhortation is a lesson in prayer. We learn to pray by praying. Jesus gave us a pattern, and Paul gave us an example. These can help us to develop our own praying. May God give us all grace to learn to pray again.

Humbly yours in Christ Jesus,
Archie Murray
Lobo, Southern Ontario

If you have been blessed by my books, please send me an email. I would love to hear from you and pray for you
archiemurray7@gmail.com

OTHER BOOKS IN THE SERIES:

There are three books in this series so far. Although they are stand-alone books, they do form one discussion on prayer. The series adheres to the natural flow of Jesus's teaching on prayer found in the Sermon on the Mount.

The Room: Preparation for Prayer
The Room serves as a prologue to the Lord's Prayer. Often we forget to prepare and instead rush in where angels fear to tread. Jesus tells us to go into our room!

The Pattern: The Lord's Prayer
The Pattern is the actual text of The Lord's Prayer, which is the most used, most abused, and most ignored prayer in the Bible. In this book, the prayer is explained and expanded upon.

The Practice: Paul's Prayers in Ephesians
The Practice provides an example of real prayer as found in Paul's prayers in Ephesians. There Paul tells his readers what he actually prays for when praying for them.

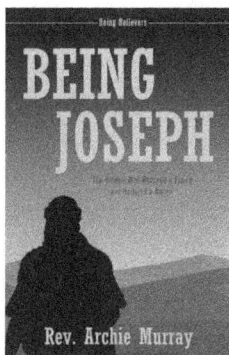

Being Joseph (978-1-4866-1573-5)
Have you ever felt betrayed by a family member? Have you ever needed even a glimpse of hope to help you through a tough situation? In the Old Testament, we read that Joseph was thrown into a pit and then sold by his own brothers. This great betrayal left him feeling alone and in despair. Unfortunately, this was only the beginning of his troubles.

Being Joseph takes a closer, pastoral perspective on perseverance through hardships, the value of forgiveness even when it's near impossible, and the redemptive hope of reconciliation. Joseph's story expands on dreams, slavery, seduction, imprisonment, and the restoration of a family. In the worst moments of Joseph's life, we can see that God never left his side. The lessons we can learn from this book can help enrich our daily lives in this difficult world today.

All ages will benefit from this captivating commentary on a real family, just like yours.

BEING RUTH

Rev. Archie Murray

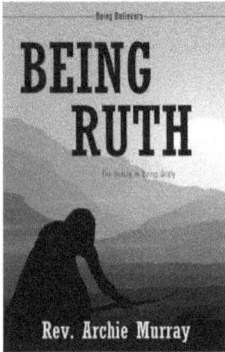

Being Ruth (978-1-4866-1709-8)

Have you ever felt like your faith was being tested? Have you ever experienced the death of a loved one? The book of Ruth, found in the Old Testament, is a moving story of a sad tragedy followed by an unrelenting commitment, both human and divine. Ruth's sadness is followed by hope deferred, yet undeterred.

Being Ruth takes a closer pastoral perspective on the shape of human expressions and relationships, the significance of names, and the consequences of men dying childless. We see Ruth, the committed daughter-in-law to Naomi, responding with grace during a difficult time in life. Although this is not your typical love story, as you allow the Scriptures to speak you'll find a beautifully enchanting story.

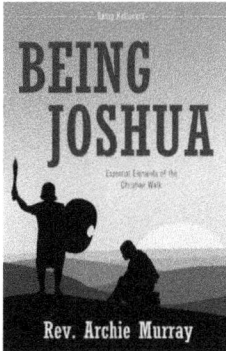

Being Joshua (978-1-4866-2213-9)

Have you ever wanted to be stronger, more vibrant, as a believer? Have you ever felt the church is weak when it should be strong? Have you ever felt that rampant evil should be shut down? Do you believe change is possible in the world, in the church… in you?! Joshua experienced a bad start in life—forty years in slavery. He wandered a desert for another forty years. Yet it was in and from these experiences that he discovered the believer's strength. He escaped slavery and went on to shut evil down and conquer the Promised Land. If we want to conquer the world for God… we must allow God first to conquer us.

Being Joshua shows how God uses the circumstances of life to change us into who He wants us to be. In life's slavery and wanderings, Joshua teaches us how to synapse with God's Spirit. Joshua teaches us that God is doing something—we are a part of it, but it is bigger than us. Joshua teaches us how to view life within the purposes of God and gain victory over our circumstances and ultimately ourselves. Joshua shows us that the weakest and the strongest believers need to encourage themselves and be strong. He reminds us, pertinent to our times, that we must also encourage each other. Joshua learned this from the Old Testament Scriptures taught in a godly family life, a community of believers, and a personal walk of faith in God. His education was by words and examples in real daily life. This book is written from a pastoral and practical perspective.